Original title:
The Magic of Christmas Eve

Copyright © 2024 Creative Arts Management OÜ
All rights reserved.

Author: Natalia Harrington
ISBN HARDBACK: 978-9916-90-964-5
ISBN PAPERBACK: 978-9916-90-965-2

Whispers of Winter's Night

The snowflakes dance, a clumsy show,
As squirrels slip on ice like a pro.
Frosty breath makes clouds of white,
While hot cocoa's the drink of the night.

A snowman grins, a carrot nose,
He'll crack a joke, I suppose.
But watch out for that snowball fight,
Do run fast, it's quite a sight!

Starlit Dreams in Feathery Snow

Under the stars, the flakes will gleam,
Little kids plot their snowy dream.
Build a fort, a kingdom tall,
Until someone makes it fall.

With mittens on and cheeks so red,
Giggling as they tumble, they fled.
Snow angels lie, spread out with glee,
While mom yells, 'Get back here, not on me!'

Twilight's Embrace: A Festive Tale

Twilight comes with sparkly lights,
As carolers sing with pitchy sights.
The tree stands proud, with baubles bright,
But the cat just swatted it, all right!

Cousins gather with tales galore,
Eating cookies, then asking for more.
Uncle's jokes make the room feel warm,
Even if they have zero charm.

Secrets Beneath the Mistletoe

Under the boughs, a secret's spun,
A kiss, a giggle, oh what fun!
But Uncle Bob's got a funny tale,
It leads to laughter that'll never pale.

A tight-lipped grin, a wink, a dance,
While Grandma rolls her eyes at romance.
The mistletoe has tricks in store,
Like peeking cousins that ask for more!

The Night the World Stood Still

The cat jumped high, caught the moon,
The dog chased it, barking a tune.
The neighbors peered from their cozy dens,
Thinking this party would never end.

A squirrel stole snacks, oh what a sight,
Dancing on roofs, in the pale moonlight.
The world was frozen, gawked in surprise,
As chaos ruled under starry skies.

A cow on a skateboard, a goat on a bike,
Who knew they'd have such talent to strike?
With giggles and gaffes, we all stood still,
The night was alive with ridiculous thrill.

A Christmas Tale Beneath the Boughs

Santa got stuck in the chimney last year,
The reindeer all giggled, spread Christmas cheer.
The cookies were gone, he had none to munch,
So he fashioned a plan, for a late-night brunch.

Elves wrapped the gifts with tape on their ears,
The cat swatted bows, spreading small cheers.
The tree leaned to one side, lights tangled tight,
Yet nobody cared, it felt just right.

A snowman emerged, with a carrot nose,
Wearing sunglasses, striking a pose.
Cocoa in hand, we laughed till we cried,
Under the lights, joy spread far and wide.

Twinkling Lights in the Winter's Embrace

The lights blinked wildly, like they'd lost their way,
Flickering brightly, in a colorful array.
Neighbors all gathered, shaking their heads,
"Who needs a tree when the gutter's well-fed?"

The snowflakes danced down, it was quite a show,
Land on a nose, then slide off with a glow.
Kids built a snowman as tall as a fence,
With bits of old cabbage, it made no sense.

In cozy warm jackets, we trudged through the frost,
With hot chocolate spoons, we were never lost.
Laughter erupted, hiding our shivers,
In winter's embrace, joy wrapped us like rivers.

The Gift of Wonder and Belief

A tiny girl whispered with dreams in her eyes,
"Is magic just real? Or just in the skies?"
Her teddy bear nodded, a wink and a grin,
"Let's dash through the snow, let the fun times begin!"

While Father Time snoozed in his recliner chair,
A dragon flew past, the wind in her hair.
They giggled and plotted a journey so grand,
To the land of sweets, made of gingerbread sand.

As night kissed the earth, stars began to gleam,
The world held its breath, as if in a dream.
With wishes and wonders wrapped up in delight,
The gift of belief shone oh so bright!

The Slumbering Town Wrapped in White

The town is snuggled in a quilt,
The snowflakes fall without a guilt.
Everyone's dreams are fluffy and light,
While squirrels plan a snowball fight.

The roofs are heavy, the cars are stuck,
The mailman shouts, 'Oh, what luck!'
Children build forts, oh what a mess,
While their parents sip cocoa, feeling blessed.

Tales Told by the Crackling Fire

Gather 'round, it's story time,
Where laughter comes and woes decline.
Uncle Joe starts with his tall tales,
Of pirates and storms and wind-filled sails.

Grandma winks, says she knows best,
Of the roasted chestnuts, she'll never rest.
Everyone munches, the fire pops bright,
As shadows dance and spirits ignite.

Snowbound Reveries Under Moonlit Skies

The moonbeams twinkle, the stars do sway,
Snowmen gossip about the day.
A snow angel flaps with feathery grace,
While penguins waddle, leading the race.

Hot cocoa fumes rise in the air,
As mittens and scarves become a pair.
Sleds zoom by with whoops and squeals,
In this snowy land, joy reveals.

A Flicker of Joy in the Quiet Dark

The candles flicker, shadows prance,
As we indulge in a silly dance.
With every step, laughter ascends,
Even the cat snickers at our bends.

The night is calm, yet hearts are loud,
As we embrace like a fluffy cloud.
In this quiet dark, joy finds a spark,
While we freeze the moments, like a quirky lark.

Lullabies of the Winter's Heart

Snowflakes dance on a chilly breeze,
They tickle your nose and make you sneeze.
Hot cocoa spills on a woolly sock,
Frosty fingers tickle the clock.

Snowmen smile with carrot noses,
Waving sticks like winter poses.
While penguins slide down icy slopes,
Singing sweet tunes of snowy hopes.

Secrets Beneath the Evergreen Canopy

Whispers of squirrels in a leafy chat,
Planning their heists for the winter fat.
Under the boughs where pine cones rest,
They hold the secrets of nature's fest.

The owls hoot in their wise old way,
Debating who's squirrel-scratching today.
While branches sway with playful grace,
Winter's secrets dance and embrace.

The Embrace of Winter's Warmth

Blankets hug like a soft, warm hug,
As hot tea steams like a friendly mug.
Chilly noses meet a crackling fire,
Where marshmallows melt like a sweet desire.

In woolly socks, we shuffle and slide,
With giggles echoing, joy can't hide.
Winter's embrace is snug and bright,
Even when days are shorter than night.

Envelopes of Joy on Starry Nights

Stars wink down from a velvet sky,
Painting your dreams where snowflakes fly.
With laughter wrapped in a frosty bow,
We pull up our blankets and watch the glow.

Snowball fights send giggles high,
As frosty breath makes clouds that sigh.
Joy wraps us tight like a cozy song,
In winter's embrace, we all belong.

Moonlit Wishes on Whispering Winds

Under a moon so bright and round,
I wished for pizza, what a sound!
Whispers of cheese danced in the night,
While stars giggled with pure delight.

The wind carried dreams, oh what a tease,
I asked for chocolate, if you please!
Instead came pickles, sour and green,
I laughed so hard, you should've seen!

A laugh in the breeze, the moon did cheer,
As I twirled about with no fear.
Wishes and giggles flew high and low,
In moonlit magic, our dreams would grow.

So next time you wish, just keep it light,
Or you might end up with a flying kite!
For in this night, with whimsy and glee,
Dreams come alive, just wait and see!

The Palette of Joyful Colors

In a land where rainbows painted the sky,
I tried to paint my hat, oh my!
It turned out red with polka dots,
A sight that only laughter got.

Blues and greens danced on my cheeks,
While yellow ducklings played hide and seek.
I spilled some orange, the squished kind,
Now my dog thinks I've lost my mind!

The palette spun with giggles and cheer,
As purple cows started to steer.
I painted the grass with shades of pink,
And I swear it started to blink!

With every stroke, a new laugh arose,
Painting my world, anything goes!
So grab your brush, let colors unfurl,
In this joyful mess, we'll change the world!

Frosty Fables by the Hearth

By the fire, we gather round,
With frosty tales that know no bound.
The snowflakes whisper secrets untold,
While marshmallows dance, oh so bold!

A snowman frowned, his nose went miss,
He lost his scarf, oh what a kiss!
With every freeze, new tales would pop,
Hot cocoa spills, but we never stop.

The winds recite their frosty verse,
As blankets wrap us, oh what a curse!
But no need to fret, for laughter inside,
Keeps the chill out, it's our merry ride.

So gather 'round for stories so grand,
With laughter and warmth, we take a stand.
In frosty fables, joy takes flight,
As we dream by the hearth, all through the night!

The Nighttime Canvas of Dreams

On a canvas of dreams, stars splatter wide,
I painted a cat with a whimsical stride.
He wore a top hat, with a twinkle and spin,
In a world where all nonsense can truly begin.

A dog on a skateboard zoomed past my nose,
Chasing the moon, oh how it glows!
And unicorns danced in a glittery show,
As I painted with laughter, just letting it flow.

Each brushstroke sparkled with all that I feel,
Like pancakes flying—a wonderful meal!
In the quiet of night, my dreams take a leap,
As I giggle and paint before going to sleep.

So close your eyes, let your canvas collide,
With colors of joy, let imagination guide.
For in this night, where absurd is supreme,
You'll find your own magic in the tapestry of dreams!

Dreams Carried on a Gentle Breeze

I caught a dream on a breeze,
It whispered sweetly with such ease.
But then it turned and flew away,
Chasing it made me late today.

I saw it dance among the trees,
Doing the cha-cha with the bees.
I thought I'd join, but tripped and fell,
Now I just laugh and wish it well.

I asked the wind to bring it back,
It chuckled loud and changed its track.
Now I sip tea and wave goodbye,
To dreams that float like clouds in the sky.

But who needs dreams when snacks are near?
I'll trade a wish for a slice of cheer.
With cookies crumbled in my lap,
I find my joy in this little nap.

The Night of Endless Possibilities

It's a night full of dreams, oh what luck!
I tried to dance, but I ran out of pluck.
With my two left feet, I spun and slipped,
Into the punch bowl, I awkwardly dipped.

The stars above giggled, they saw my plight,
As I splashed around in the moon's soft light.
I raised my glass, a toast to the fall,
To nights like these, where I can stall.

I pondered if I could fly to the moon,
But my head was spinning, my thoughts a cartoon.
So I made a wish on a flying cake,
Prayed the frosting wouldn't make me awake.

In endless possibilities, I find my cheer,
Like wearing mismatched socks, oh dear!
So let's embrace the silly and bright,
For every flop just makes it all right.

Frosted Fairytales Come to Life

Once upon a frosty night,
A snowman danced, oh what a sight!
He twirled and spun with glee galore,
Until his carrot nose hit the floor.

Oh dear, oh my, what a frosty fate,
A snowman's dance was destined for debate.
With a hat that flew into the air,
His frozen friends just sat and stared.

They built a snow horse with a shiny mane,
But when it moved, they screamed in vain.
"Life's a blast when frozen in time!"
They shouted out, covered in slime.

So if you see a fairy tale,
Remember the snowman's frosty flail.
Because in frost and laughter alike,
We find the magic, oh, what a spike!

Radiance in the Stillness

In the stillness of the night,
A glow-worm buzzed, oh what a fright!
It called to crickets, "Come join the fun!"
But they just chirped, "We're all outrun!"

The moon rolled its eyes, reflecting light,
As fireflies gathered for their flight.
They blinked and winked in a silly line,
Twirling around like they'd drunk too much wine.

A cloud sneezed loud, such a silly show,
"Bless you!" we cried, "Now, let's all glow!"
In the glow of laughter, we found our place,
Radiance in stillness, a goofy embrace.

So if you find stillness on a night bright,
Join in the fun and take a bite.
Of laughter, glow, and silly dreams,
In stillness, we shine; it's not as it seems.

The Night the World Held its Breath

The clock struck twelve, the cat went mad,
The aliens danced with a bumbling lad.
The stars fell down, but they weren't too bright,
They lit up the world, what a crazy sight!

A giraffe in pajamas played hopscotch with glee,
While elephants balanced on top of a tree.
The moon wore a hat, quite comical too,
As everyone wondered just what they should do!

They tiptoed around on spaghetti so long,
And a cow joined the choir, oh, how they sang wrong!
With laughter resounding, all worries took flight,
That night, the world held its breath with delight!

So if you hear whispers of antics so grand,
Just remember that night when silliness planned.
With dreams danced away, and joy on full spread,
A world once so weighty, by laughter was fed.

A Canvas of Frost and Starlight

A painter arrived with a brush made of ice,
He dipped it in starlight, how perfectly nice!
He swirled up a moonbeam and sprinkled some frost,
Creating a landscape where nothing was lost!

The trees wore tuxedos, the squirrels donned ties,
While snowflakes escaped on a whimsy surprise.
A penguin in sneakers put on quite the dance,
As winter grinned wide, offering a chance!

A deer in a bowtie played chess with a fox,
While rabbits in slippers spilled milk from their blocks.
With laughter a-rolling, the night softly sang,
In a harmony charming, where joy brightly rang!

As magic was spun on this canvas quite bright,
The world held its breath in the glow of the night.
For in every cold moment, warmth can be found,
In the play of the frost, where joy knows no bound.

Sugarplum Fantasies and Snowflake Kisses

In dreams of sugarplums, we twirled around,
With chocolate riverbanks and candy cane ground.
A snowflake named Flurry proposed a grand ball,
Inviting all creatures, both big and both small!

The bears wore bright tutus, the owls had a blast,
While bunnies played violins, oh, how they danced fast!
The marshmallow clouds floated under the moon,
As stars whispered secrets to the sweet afternoon.

With marshmallow cups filled with cocoa divine,
And peppermint sticks made to sweeten the rhyme.
A pie-flavored comet zoomed by with a wink,
As we laughed and we partied, no time left to think!

In sugarplum fantasies, we spun through the night,
Sharing snowflake kisses, our hearts feeling light.
For in this sweet dreamland where laughter persists,
Is a festival of joy, none can resist!

Celestial Melodies Softly Unfurled

Underneath the vastness where star breezes glide,
The moon played the piano, with nothing to hide.
The planets all gathered in fanciful tune,
While comets flew by, making wishes to swoon!

A chorus of crickets sung sweet symphonies,
With fireflies blinking like bright melodies.
The galaxies swayed, doing the twist and the turn,
While meteors zipped past with lessons to learn!

The sun sent a ray with a trumpet-like blast,
Encouraging dreams, for the night wouldn't last.
It called out to starlight, "Let's jam on the go!"
As cosmic confetti began to overflow!

In this concert of wonders, where laughter ascends,
Each star was a note that time brilliantly bends.
So close your eyes tight, let the music swirl,
In celestial melodies, the universe twirled!

Celestial Journeys on Frosted Paths

On a slippery slope with stars aglow,
I slipped on a comet and fell in the snow.
My sled was a rocket, it's true as it seems,
I zoomed past the moon, chasing wild, wacky dreams.

With frostbite on fingers, I boldly declared,
That penguins in space really may not be scared.
They floated on icebergs, sipping hot cocoa,
While I chased a shooting star, feeling quite low.

The North Pole's a party, they dance with delight,
Elves jigging with snowmen all shimmering bright.
But I tripped on a snowdrift, oh what a sight,
And vanished in snowflakes—gone, out of sight.

Now frozen in laughter, I chuckle and muse,
That journeys in winter can't help but amuse.
For each slip and each fall's just a laugh at the end,
In celestial realms, all the frostballs are friends.

Lanterns of Hope in the Dark

In the heart of the night, when shadows do play,
A lantern lit up, chasing darkness away.
With giggles and whispers, the fireflies dance,
While I trip on my shoelace, who's giving me a chance?

The owls hoot in rhythm, they join in the fun,
While bats join the party, 'Hey, look how I run!'
We roast marshmallows on a stick made of dreams,
While plotting to steal all the moon's yummy beams.

The stars wink in laughter, they twinkle with glee,
As I spark a flashlight, yelling, "Look at me!"
But a raccoon chortles, "That's not how it's done,
You're lighting the woods up, let's dash and then run!"

With lanterns of hope that twinkle so bright,
We'll dance till the dawn, chasing off the night.
For even in darkness, we find every spark,
And sing to the world, we're the light in the dark!

Crystals of Joy in a Whispered Breeze

In a garden of laughter, with petals so bright,
I spun round in joy, oh what a delight!
Crystals of giggles, they glimmer and shine,
As bees buzz around like they've had too much wine.

The flowers are chatting, their secrets they share,
While I trip on the daisies without any care.
A rainbow appears as the sun starts to rise,
With chirps from the birdies, oh what a surprise!

In whispers of breezes, the laughter takes flight,
As butterflies wobble, what a comical sight!
They land on my nose, and what can I say?
I sneeze in surprise, sending them on their way!

Yet joy blooms around me, like a colorful feast,
With giggles and sparkles, oh laughter released.
For each crystal of joy is a moment to seize,
In a garden of fun, where worries just freeze.

Lullabies from the Fir Tree

Under the fir tree, where soft shadows play,
A squirrel sings sweetly, inviting the day.
With acorns for percussion, they tap on the bark,
While the crickets join in, in the sweet summer dark.

A bear hums a tune, oh what a rough sound,
While a raccoon's rummaging, turning the ground.
The frogs croak a gentle, forgetful refrain,
As lullabies echo like a soft, silly train.

In the whispers of leaves, the breezes entwine,
With dreams of the forest that swirl and combine.
Like silly old owls in their nightgown parade,
Their wisdom is quirky, like a grand masquerade.

So cuddle in close, let the night drift away,
With lullabies soft, by the old fir tree sway.
For among the odd critters and tunes in the dark,
We'll dream up adventures, together, embark!

The Palette of Cheer and Calm

In the morning light, I sip my tea,
A splash of cream, just for glee.
Pastels dance across the wall,
My socks are bright, I'm having a ball!

A canvas of joy, I paint my day,
With laughter and giggles, come what may.
Each brushstroke a chuckle, a twist, a grin,
The masterpiece glimmers, let the fun begin!

Colorful socks, a tie that's bold,
My wardrobe's a story that never gets old.
With a wink and a nod, I strut with flair,
Spreading cheer is my job, I swear!

So grab your palette, let's mix some fun,
In the gallery of life, we've just begun.
With hues of laughter, let's paint the scene,
A world bright and cheerful, oh so serene!

Rumblings of Laughter in Winter's Grip

Snowflakes are falling, the ground's covered white,
But who needs warmth when you've got snowball fight?
Laughter erupts like a cracking tree,
As we tumble and roll, setting jokes free!

Hot cocoa's brewing, marshmallows afloat,
Sipping and giggling, we laugh 'til we bloat.
The icicles drip, they seem to agree,
That winter's a canvas for joy and esprit!

A snowman stands guard with a carrot nose,
Wink at him lightly, oh how he knows!
With a scarf made of laughter, and eyes all aglow,
In the chill of the season, our happiness shows!

So let winter's grip bring its icy delight,
We'll dance in the snow, hearts warm and light.
With rumblings of laughter, we banish the cold,
In this frosty wonderland, our joys unfold!

The Pulse of Hope in Chill of Night

Stars are twinkling like cheeky sprites,
While I'm wrapped snugly, avoiding the bites!
The moon whispers secrets, quite bold and bright,
Nudging my heart with its shimmering light.

In the still of the night, the world seems to cheer,
Whispers of laughter are all that I hear.
So I'll dance in my socks, take off my frown,
For every chill moment, hope won't let down!

A frosty breeze tickles my nose,
I giggle aloud, as my happiness grows.
Each breath is a shimmer, a twinkling spark,
Glowing with promise, igniting the dark!

So even in winter, when skies wear a frown,
The pulse of hope beats, it'll never drown.
With laughter and dreams, we'll create our way,
Through the chill of the night, come what may!

Heartfelt Conceits on Frosty Breezes

Oh frosty breezes, whispers of chill,
You tease my cheeks and give me a thrill.
With hats on our heads, we prance and we play,
Sipping on cider, making snow angels sway!

The world's a white wonder, I can't help but grin,
As snowflakes settle, my cheeky heart spins.
The icicles jiggle, conspiring with me,
To laugh at the winter, wild and free!

With cheeky remarks, I banter with snow,
Every chilly gust, I embrace with a glow.
The frost whispers secrets, seasoned with fun,
In heartfelt conceits, we race 'til we're done!

So let's cherish the cold with laughter and cheer,
In frosty breezes, I'll hold you most dear.
With joy in our hearts and a giggle or two,
We'll weather the winter, just me and you!

Secrets Shared by the Frosted Moon

Under the moon, frost bites the ground,
Whispers of secrets are softly found.
Snowflakes giggle, they dance in delight,
While rabbits wear coats that are too tight.

Icicles hang like nature's own teeth,
Wishing for hot cocoa to warm every heath.
The trees are gossiping, shaking their leaves,
About the snowman who still believes.

Bunnies and foxes are sneaking around,
Playing a game of 'who makes no sound.'
The moon is a witness, its glow so bright,
To antics of critters who play through the night.

Frosted the world in a sparkling glow,
Laughter and chuckles, all winter's show.
Secrets are shared in the crisp frosty air,
'Til morning arrives, with none left to share.

Wishes Wrapped in Silver Ribbons

Beneath twinkling stars, a wish takes flight,
Wrapped in a ribbon, shimmering bright.
Dancing on breezes, it curves and it sways,
Hoping for magic in funny, wild ways.

A cat in a hat dreams of catching a fish,
While a dog in a bowtie just wants a good dish.
Rabbits are hopping with hopes that they'll find,
Carrots that grow in abundance, well-timed.

An elf with a quirk has a joke up his sleeve,
He crafts silly wishes that trickle like leaves.
Beneath the moon's glow, laughter abounds,
As wishes swirl round in whimsical sounds.

So gather your dreams, wrap them up tight,
Embrace the absurd, let your heart take flight.
For wishes untangled bring giggles and cheer,
In this wacky world where humor's sincere.

A Chorus of Elves at Dusk

When dusk settles softly, the elves start to sing,
With tiny guitars, they strum and they swing.
A mishap with strings, one's hat flies away,
While another takes bows like it's all a ballet.

They're tangled in laughter, not caring a bit,
For mischief and giggles just help them commit.
One elf does a jig that's both wild and sweet,
While another just trips on his own little feet.

A chorus of chortles wraps 'round the tall trees,
As fairies join in, dancing light as a breeze.
With sparkles and wishes, the night fills with light,
As elves serenade the soon-to-be night.

So if you hear giggles beneath ev'ry star,
Know that the elves are just playing bizarre.
With a wink and a nudge, they escape to the dark,
Leaving behind all their laughter—a spark!

Frosted Windows and Warm Hearts

Through frosted windows, the world looks so bright,
While inside, we gather with cocoa in sight.
With marshmallows floating, the giggles ensue,
As we toast to the warmth that the hot drinks imbue.

Snowflakes are falling, like feathers in flight,
While outside, the snowmen are ready to fight.
But we stay cozy, in blankets galore,
Making snowmen jokes, then we laugh 'til we're sore.

The wind whispers secrets to trees standing tall,
While we share our stories, both silly and small.
The warmth of our hearts keeps the chill at bay,
As the outside world sparkles in winter's ballet.

So gather your friends, let the laughter ring clear,
Frosted windows won't freeze the love we hold dear.
In moments of joy, let's cherish the part,
Of warmth within, and frost on the heart.

A Symphony of Joy and Light

When I dance with my socks on,
I slide across the floor.
My cat gives me the side-eye,
Like I'm a total bore.

Every time I bake cookies,
Flour dust is in the air.
I'm always stuck with chocolate,
Right in my nose and hair.

The music blasts at midnight,
We groove like we're the best.
But then I trip on my shoelace,
And tumble like the rest.

So raise a glass of pickle juice,
Let's toast to silly cheer.
Life's a symphony of sounds,
Mostly laughter, never fear!

Shadows Dancing on Snowy Streets

The snowman's hat is missing,
Did the raccoons attack?
His carrot's leaning sideways,
Looks like he's got a knack.

Footprints lead to nowhere,
Where did my dog escape?
He's plotting with the snowflakes,
In a winter wonder shape.

Snowballs fly like cannonballs,
Whizzing through the air.
I duck and dodge my own fail,
As I slip in my despair.

But laughter fills the frosty night,
With friends around in glee.
These dancing shadows in the snow,
Are the best company.

A Festive Heartbeat Beneath the Stars

When twinkling lights are hanging,
I trip over the cord.
My neighbors laugh and giggle,
As I give them my best snore.

The tree is leaning sideways,
With ornaments askew.
I swear the star's just winking,
It knows what I will do.

With hot cocoa in our hands,
We dance beneath the moon.
But spilled it on my sweater,
Now it smells like marshmallow doom.

Yet still we sing our carols loud,
With laughter in the air.
A festive heartbeat in our chests,
Who cares if I'm a bear?

The Storyteller's Song of Winter Nights

Gather round, my friends, so dear,
I've tales of winter nights.
Of penguins in tuxedos,
And all their frosty fights.

Once I tried to bake a pie,
But baked a giant flop.
The dog got to the chocolate,
Now he won't stop to hop.

The fire crackles sweetly,
As shadows dance around.
I'm sure I saw a gnome pass by,
With candy canes he found.

So snuggle close, and let me spin,
These stories full of cheer.
For winter nights are warmer,
With laughter loud and near.

Ember Glow and Skyward Whispers

The fire crackles, pops and sings,
As marshmallows dance on goofy strings.
The logs are log-jammed in a hug,
While we all sip on cocoa, snug as a bug.

But wait, a squirrel joins in the fun,
His acorn stash weighs a ton!
He takes a leap, grabs a twig,
And suddenly, he's doing a jig!

The stars above blink their delight,
As we howl at the moon, what a silly sight!
The embers glow like tiny stars,
As laughter travels near and far.

So here's to moments, crazy and bright,
When all our worries take flight.
With friends and fun, under moon's soft glow,
Life's a comedy, just let it flow!

The Promise of Tomorrow Beneath the Snow

Snowflakes fall like fluffy dreams,
And kids outside are filled with screams.
They build their forts, like little kings,
While mom sips tea and quietly sings.

The dog jumps in, goes belly-first,
He thinks he's found his wintry thirst!
But what he finds is cold, not hot,
And rolls around like it's his spot.

Tomorrow's sun is sneaking near,
To melt the snow, that's what I fear!
But till then, let's make snowmen tall,
With carrots for noses, standing proud and all.

So here's to winters, with laughter and cheer,
As snow will vanish, spring draws near.
Let's treasure the cold, hold on tight,
For warm hugs await, come morning light!

Twilight's Gift of Wonder and Warmth

The sun dips low, the sky's aglow,
As the twilight dances, soft and slow.
A squirrel with style struts across the way,
With shades on, he's ruling the day!

The crickets chirp a twilight tune,
While fireflies blink like stars in June.
They light the path where we all roam,
In search of ice cream, we call it home!

The skies turn pink, then purple too,
As night wraps around like a warm, soft shoe.
We roast marshmallows and tell silly tales,
While memories dance like firefly trails.

So raise a toast to twilight's glory,
For in this moment, we're all the story!
Let laughter ring as stars appear,
In this dreamy place where all is clear!

Silent Whispers of Winter's Night

The world is still, wrapped up tight,
As snow drapes softly, pure and white.
A snowman grins with a carrot nose,
Hoping his frosty fashion shows!

The moon shines down, a curious spy,
As kids with sleds zip by, oh my!
They race and tumble, giggle and squeal,
With cheeks so red, oh, what a deal!

Hot cocoa waits, like a warm embrace,
As winter whispers, "Join the chase!"
We gather 'round, all snug and bright,
Each sip is sweet on this cozy night.

So here's to winter, cold and grand,
With magic nestled in every hand.
Let laughter ring and hearts take flight,
In the silent whispers of winter's night!

The Thumbprint of Time on Frost

Frosty windows hide my face,
As I search for my long-lost grace.
Time's thumbprint smudged, oh dear,
It seems I've lost my winter cheer.

Jumpsuits from the past, oh wow,
Why did I think I'd rock them now?
Sipping cocoa, bad jokes on blast,
At least my memories are a blast!

The snowflakes fall, looking so neat,
Except when they land on my seat!
I slip and slide like a clumsy seal,
Oh, how this winter makes me squeal!

So here's to times both good and bad,
Frosty days that make me glad.
Embrace the laughs, let worries slide,
With a thumbprint of time as my guide.

Embers that Dance with Memories

Embers flicker, stories unfold,
Tales of mishaps we loved to be told.
Marshmallows roast to a golden hue,
While I ponder the dumb things I do.

S'mores in hand, I bite too fast,
Now my tongue's a blistered cast.
Laughter erupts, oh what a sight,
As I dance away from the blazing light!

Ghost stories shared under starry skies,
Just to hear my buddy's sleepy sighs.
"Did you hear that?" I whisper with dread,
He's fast asleep, dreaming of bread!

With every crackle, a chuckle erupts,
In the glow of the fire, our joy erupts.
Memories warm like a cozy old quilt,
As we relive the laughter we built.

Winter's Embrace: A Night Like No Other

Winter nights with a frosty bite,
Wrapped in blankets, all snug and tight.
The wind howls, a song so sweet,
While I let out a shivering squeak!

Carving snowmen with silly hats,
While they plot to attack the cats.
I slip on ice, a graceful fall,
And land right next to my neighbor's dog, Paul.

Hot cocoa in hand, my optimism high,
But I tripped on a squirrel and said goodbye.
The snow-packed paths, all swirly and curled,
I think winter might have me twirled!

With frosty breath and laughter so bright,
Winter's embrace, a heartwarming sight.
Embrace the chaos, let nothing disband,
For nights like this are simply grand!

Boundless Wonders Beneath the Stars

Stars above, they wink and shine,
While I contemplate the cosmic line.
"Why is the sky so full of glee?"
I ponder seriously, spilling my tea!

Aliens watching, sipping their drinks,
Oh wait, that's just my neighbor who thinks.
With a telescope that's broken at best,
He claims he's seen creatures way out west!

Questions arise like popcorn in air,
"Did dinosaurs ever put on a fair?"
With each chuckle beneath the moon's beam,
We craft the wildest of dreams, it seems.

So here beneath these stellar jewels,
Let's gather the laughter, and break all the rules.
For wonders await in the vast night sky,
Boundless adventures as we aim high!

Nightfall's Caress: A Celebration of Peace

As the sun dips low and takes a break,
The moon yawns wide with a sleepy shake.
Stars flip pancakes in the sky so blue,
While the night whispers, "Hey, I'm here for you!"

Squirrels in pajamas dance on the lawn,
Chasing shadows until the early dawn.
The owls hoot jokes, an elegant crew,
Every night's a party, just for you!

Lampshades twinkle with a friendly glow,
Even the crickets have a comedy show.
Under the cover of night's soft embrace,
Let's celebrate peace with a silly face!

So raise a toast with mugs of moonlight,
And laugh 'til your belly feels just right.
In this serene hour, let's all unwind,
For nightfall's caress is simply divine!

The Anticipation of Joyful Hearts

When morning breaks with a sunbeam's kiss,
Anticipation builds for a day of bliss.
Coffee's brewing, oh, what a treat,
Dance around the kitchen, shuffle your feet!

The mailbox squeaks, what could it be?
A letter from distant relatives, whee!
More cat videos and photos galore,
This is the joy that we all adore.

The school bell rings, kids dash about,
With laughter and smiles, they squeal and shout.
Lunchboxes squeak, trading snacks in a rush,
Life is a party, oh, feel that rush!

Joyful hearts leap like bunnies in spring,
Ready to embrace what the day may bring.
So grab your pals and share some cheer,
For today is magical, that's crystal clear!

Stars Cascading Like Glittering Wishes

Stars twinkle brightly with a wink and a grin,
A sparkling cascade, let the wishing begin.
Grab a handful of dreams, throw them out wide,
Let's ride on the back of a cosmic tide!

The Milky Way's like a giant ice cream cone,
Laced with sprinkles and dreams of our own.
As wishes scatter, we laugh and we cheer,
Hoping they reach the galactic frontier!

Comets zoom past, bringing giggles and glee,
With each shooting star, we shout, "Look at me!"
The universe laughs, sharing secrets in flight,
As we make wishes beneath starlit night.

So count the stars, let your heart take a chance,
Join in the cosmos for a celestial dance.
For every wish cast is a promise so sweet,
Like candy for souls, a delightful treat!

Shadows Dance in Winter's Embrace

When winter whispers with frosty delight,
Shadows come out to join in the night.
They tango and twirl on the icy ground,
Creating a symphony, chill all around!

Snowflakes waltz, a soft and white crowd,
While shadows boogie, cheering out loud.
In this frosty ballroom, we all find our place,
Embracing the chill with a grin on our face.

Hot cocoa swirls, marshmallows in flight,
As shadows and sparkles join in the night.
The snowman grins with a carrot-nosed glee,
In winter's embrace, we all feel so free!

So grab your mittens and pull on your hat,
Join the shadow dancers, let's have a chat!
For winter's a tale of laughter and grace,
With shadows that twirl in a snowy embrace!

Echoes of Laughter Through Frosty Fields

Chilly winds with a giggle,
Snowflakes dance, wiggle, and wiggle.
Sleds race down a slippery lane,
While kids shout, "Again!" with no pain.

Hot cocoa spills, oh dear me!
Marshmallows float like the sea.
Snowmen wear hats, tilted, askew,
And wave with a grin, just for you.

Dogs leap high with a snowy yip,
Chasing tails on a frosty trip.
Caught one paw in a deep snowdrift,
Now it's a snowball fight, what a gift!

And when the sun sets, evening cheers,
Echoes of laughter wrap us like peers.
Through frosty fields, we run and we play,
Creating memories that never fray.

The Nutmeg Scent of Stardust

Baking cookies, a swirl of delight,
Nutmeg sprinkles in a dance of light.
The oven hums a merry tune,
While flour clouds float like a moon.

In every pinch, a little magic,
Sweet aromas, nothing tragic.
Sticky fingers, where's the dough?
A taste test, oh what a show!

Grandma laughs, a twinkle in her eye,
"Just one more cookie, give it a try!"
Elves might complain of a sugar spree,
But nutmeg stardust is wild and free.

As plates pile high, we all take a seat,
Munching away on this tasty feat.
The laughter and crumbs, oh what a fuss,
In this kitchen, there's joy for all of us.

Starlit Paths Through Snowy Woods

Under the stars, we stroll through snow,
Twinkling lights seem to put on a show.
The crunch of boots, a rhythmic delight,
While moonbeams giggle, glowing bright.

Trees wear blankets of shimmering white,
Branches hang low, a whimsical sight.
Snowflakes whisper secrets so light,
While shadows dance, oh what a night!

A squirrel slips, gives a startled shout,
Plunges in snow, then pops right out.
We share a laugh, oh what a goof,
And frosty breaths resound like a woof!

Further along, by a glistening brook,
We spot a snow angel, give it a look.
Giggles and joy fill the starlit air,
On snowy paths, there's magic to share.

Yuletide Joy in Every Heartbeat

The tree is lit, twinkling bright,
Ornaments hung with pure delight.
Tinsel shimmers, dancing with cheer,
As carols echo from ear to ear.

The smell of cookies wafts through the hall,
Leftovers? No way! We'll munch it all.
Nutcracker soldiers guard the toys,
While laughter reigns among the girls and boys.

Wrapping presents, a tape-glue mess,
Last year's gifts? Some we won't confess!
But every ribbon, every bow,
Is tied with love, as we all know.

Yuletide joy fills every heart,
From cozy moments, we never part.
Let's raise a cup, make a toast so sweet,
To laughter and love, the perfect treat.

Enchanted Lanterns in the Snow

The lanterns flicker, oh what a sight,
They dance in the snow like stars at night.
With snowflakes giggling, a playful show,
I tripped on a drift, then shouted, "Whoah!"

The frostbitten gnome with his hat askew,
Complains about snow, says, "Not cool, dude!"
His nose turned red like a ripe cherry,
He mumbles about warmth and getting merry.

A snowman slid by on a slick little ride,
Yelling, "Who needs skis? I've got snow to glide!"
He tried a backflip, but what a flop,
And now he's just rolling, he can't seem to stop.

So let's raise a glass to the snowman crew,
With enchanted lanterns, we'll dance 'til we're blue.
In this snowy realm where laughter flows free,
Who knew winter fun could be so silly?

A Tapestry of Starry Dreams

Beneath the vast sky, the stars have a chat,
They giggle and wink, and swap tales just like that.
One's lost his way, says he's stuck in a loop,
The moon rolls his eyes, "You're a real goof troop!"

A comet zooms by with a trail of ice cream,
He shouts out, "Catch me! I've got the best dream!"
But all of the planets just laugh at his speed,
"Dreams taste much better with whipped cream, indeed!"

A twinkling star feels a tickle within,
She tries to suppress her hysterical grin.
"Let's form a conga, across the night sea!"
But her friends are too busy, just sipping their tea.

In the tapestry woven of dreams from above,
Laughter and joy fit like hand in a glove.
So we sway with the stars in the soft cosmic beams,
For every laugh shared is a star that redeems.

Candlelight Dreams Beneath the Pines

In the forest so dark, candles flicker and glow,
The shadows are dancing, putting on quite a show.
A raccoon in a hat tries to join in the fun,
But tripped on a twig and said, "I'm not done!"

A wise old owl hoots, "What a sight I see here,
A party of critters, a jubilant cheer!"
He sips on some cider, a very fine brew,
While squirrels break-dance and paint the world blue.

The pine trees whisper, sharing a laugh,
As a hedgehog rolls by, but takes a wrong path.
He lands in a puddle, with a plop and a splash,
And all of the animals giggle and dash.

Candlelight dreams are the sweetest of schemes,
For forest shenanigans brighten our dreams.
Beneath the pines' glow, let the laughter take flight,
In this whimsical forest, everything's bright!

Snowflakes Dance on Midnight Air

Snowflakes pirouette, like ballerinas do,
They flutter and tumble, a sparkling crew.
A snowman is watching with popcorn in hand,
He cheers them on loudly, "A great snowy band!"

A polar bear claps, sporting shades on his snout,
While penguins are sliding, there's laughter, no doubt.
One penguin slips, then he's gone in a flash,
And lands in a snowbank with a glorious crash!

A snowflake falls gently on a dog's fluffy nose,
He shakes it off wildly, as if it's a rose.
"Why do they dance?" he barks out with a grin,
But no one can answer, back to fun they spin.

So here's to the snowflakes, the laughter they share,
In the midnight air, spreading joy everywhere.
Let's join in their dance as the stars twinkle bright,
For laughter unites us, in this frosty night!

The Tapestry of Hope Weaved in Wonder

In a land where socks lose their pair,
Hope threads its way through the air.
It stitches dreams with a laugh,
While tired cats nap in the scarf.

With each new dawn, colors collide,
As we all try to find a ride.
Llamas dance in the morning's glow,
Wearing hats they stole from a show.

But fear not, dear friend, take a seat,
For life's a puzzle, not defeat.
Weaving giggles into our plight,
Telling tales 'til the stars are bright.

So grab a thread, let's spin a yarn,
Of miracles and a bright green fern.
In this tapestry, wild and free,
Hope laughs along, come dance with me!

A Symphony of Solitude and Cheer

In a quiet room, a cat does sing,
To the tune of an old rubber ring.
The mice tap dance on wooden floors,
While the echoing sound of boredom roars.

A teacup's waltz brings sweet delight,
Stirred by spoons in the fading light.
The wallpaper hums a soft refrain,
As the dog drools in perfect disdain.

Outside, a squirrel plays the flute,
While the mailman sports a bright pink suit.
Together we laugh, in our own little sphere,
In this symphony of solitude and cheer.

So let's raise a toast to our quirky crew,
To the moments we share, just us two.
For in the silence, there's joy to be found,
As we dance to the music, both silly and sound.

The Year's Last Whisper of Magic

As the calendar flips, we gather near,
With resolutions drowned in cheer.
Reindeer in pajamas, what a sight,
Wishing for sleep on this frosty night.

The last whisper of magic, so sly,
Hides under blankets, oh my, oh my!
The cocoa's steaming, and so are our thoughts,
As we search for the crumbs that the cookie monster spots.

With fireworks that sound like popcorn pops,
And confetti cascading like lollipops.
This year wraps up, with a chuckle and grin,
On the last of the magic, let's just dive in!

So here's to laughter and bites of delight,
To the magic that sparkles in the soft twilight.
As we bid adieu to the days running fast,
Let's wish this year's memories will forever last!

Night-Borne Secrets and Yuletide Dreams

When the clock strikes twelve with a soft chime,
The cookies are gone, oh what a crime!
Elves giggle softly, their secret so loud,
As Santa complains about the weight of his shroud.

Under the stars, stories unfold,
Of night-borne secrets and wishes untold.
Snowflakes are whispers that tickle the ground,
As the echoes of laughter swirl all around.

A snowman winks with a carrot nose,
While the moon takes selfies in subtle pose.
With each twinkle of lights, our hearts do amuse,
It's a Yuletide scene we can't help but choose.

So gather your dreams 'neath the shimmering night,
Where laughter and joy take glorious flight.
For in every secret, a treasure is found,
In night-borne stories, may happiness abound!

The Lure of Cozy Corners and Firelight

In a corner snug, where the dust bunnies play,
I hide from my chores, oh what a grand stay.
With a blanket that's fuzzy and tea that's hot,
All my adulting gets jammed in a pot.

The cat curiously hops up with a glare,
As if to say, "Why don't you get up and share?"
But who can resist this tempting delight,
When cozy corners say, 'Stay in tonight!'

I sip and I slurp, while the logs crackle loud,
Beating the cold, I'm the warmest of proud.
In my fortress of fluff and caffeine delight,
I've fought off the world—yes, I've won this fight!

So let the winds howl and the raindrops compete,
For here in my nook, life feels oh-so sweet.
With each flickering flame, my worries take flight,
In the lure of these corners, everything's right.

The Unseen Hand of Joy

I tripped on the mat, what a graceful display,
As my coffee took flight in a glorious spray.
But the giggles that followed, oh what a fine cheer,
A reminder that joy often winks, look right here!

Like a sock that goes missing—a small playful tease,
Or the dog with your sandwich, grinning with ease.
The unseen hand of joy gives twists to our fate,
Turning mundane moments to laughter so great.

When life takes a turn that feels tricky and tight,
Just whisper a riddle, or dance in the night.
With a hop and a skip, let your spirit rejoice,
For joy's just a hiccup—so listen, the voice!

So here's to the laughter, let's raise up a cheer,
For the mishaps, mistakes—oh, we hold them dear.
With each fumble and floop, embrace the own ploy,
For life's little blunders are the seeds of joy!

Anticipation Wrapped in Twilight

The sun sinks low, what a glorious sight,
Bathed in purple and crimson, it dances with light.
But while dusk settles in, there's something awry,
The ice cream truck's jingle sends me up high!

With every sweet scoop, my patience does tease,
Like waiting for Christmas—now where is my fleece?
The stars start to twinkle, my stomach's a growl,
As twilight's soft whispers bring joy on the prowl.

But alas! Here it comes, that cold creamy bliss,
The sound of the truck is pure love, not to miss.
With sprinkles and fudge, my worries take flight,
In this dreamy twilight, everything's right!

So I savor each bite as the fireflies gleam,
Wrapped in sweet hugs—oh, isn't this a dream?
As the twilight lives on, and the laughter can't halt,
I'll chase every sunset, and savor the vault!

The Glow of Hope on a Chilly Eve

On a chilly eve when the frost bites my nose,
I wrap up in layers, from my head to my toes.
As I sip on hot cocoa, it ignites such a glow,
'Tis the warmth from within that makes spirits grow.

The wind whispers tales of delightful surprise,
While the twinkling lights dance, like stars in our eyes.
With each crackle of logs that stumble and spark,
Kindling the hope that once lived in the dark.

So here by the fire, let's share silly dreams,
Of marshmallows flying and fanciful schemes.
In the warmth of the glow, as the night carries on,
We find cozy corners where laughter is born.

Though outside it's chilly, our hearts will remain,
Vividly warmed, like it's pouring with rain.
So gather together, let's echo our glee,
For the glow of hope shines brighter, you see!

The Enchantment of Flickering Lights

In the dark, they twinkle bright,
Like fireflies on a chilly night.
One's out of sync, it makes me soar,
I wonder if it's had one too many before!

The cat's in awe, eyes wide and round,
Chasing shadows all over the ground.
I lost the bulb, it rolled away,
Now it's a game—let's all just play!

Strings tangled up like spaghetti, oh dear,
The dog joins in, giving every cheer.
With a pop and a sizzle, we all jump back,
Did I mention I'm not great with the pack?

So here's to lights that sparkle and flare,
They brighten my night, with a touch of despair.
Keep flickering on, you charming display,
In this merry mess, I'll forever stay.

Frosted Wishes on Silent Air

The winter chill whispers in sighs,
Frosted wishes float in the skies.
I built a snowman, tall and stout,
With a carrot nose that's kinda clout!

He shimmies and shakes, a frosty dance,
Accidentally gave my hat a glance.
A bird stopped by, tried to take a peep,
And stole my snowman's scarf in one leap!

Hot cocoa's steaming, marshmallows dive,
But sip it too quick? You'll barely survive.
A contest for snowballs, I might just lose,
Too many slips, now I'm stuck in a snooze!

As icicles dangle, all twinkling bright,
My frosted wishes bring endless delight.
In this wintry wonder, let laughter transpire,
With friends and hot drinks that warm the desire.

Echoes of Laughter in December

Oh the laughter that rings in the air,
Like reindeer giggles—here and there!
Grandma tells tales, her yarns unravel,
While cousin Joe pretends to travel!

Stockings are hung, with snacks and sweets,
But watch out carefully for little feet.
The cookies vanish, who can we blame?
Was it Santa, or just the dog to blame?

Gift wrap confetti? It's all over me!
Like a confetti explosion, can't you see?
We trip and we tumble as we all cheer,
More laughter, more joy, it's the best time of year!

So raise a cheer for each giggle and grin,
In the echoes of laughter, let merriment spin.
December brings magic, with joy on the rise,
Catch the moments, they're the biggest surprise!

A Hearth's Glow: Warmth Among Stars

Gather round the hearth, so bright,
While shadows perform a dance of delight.
The fire crackles, sending sparks up high,
Why'd the marshmallow cross the fire? To fly!

We roast and toast, with snacks galore,
But someone always wants just one more!
The cat leaps in, steals a hot dog,
Now it's a race—let's catch the smug hog!

The stars peek in, 'Hello, how are you?'
With stories and dreams, we weave our view.
They twinkle in laughter with cosmic glee,
As we share our hopes by the log's sweet decree.

So here we are, in warmth they bless,
Amongst giggles and flames, we find our rest.
In this cozy nook, let the world fade away,
With hearts that glow, we'll savor the day!

The Whimsy of Winter's Embrace

Snowflakes dance in a joyful trance,
Building snowmen with a goofy glance.
Hot cocoa spills as we laugh and play,
Winter's silliness, come what may.

Socks on the line, a sight so rare,
Frostbite nips at my frozen hair.
Icicles hang like teeth in a grin,
Oh, what mischief this chill brings in!

Slipping and sliding on icy lanes,
A snowball fight that never wanes.
Chasing shadows of frosty breath,
Winter's humor defies all death.

Giggling kids with cheeks so bright,
Under the stars, they shine with delight.
Beneath moonlight, the world's a game,
Winter's whimsy is never the same.

Nightfall Brings Glimmers and Cheer

As sunset fades, the twilight glows,
The world dons sparkles, as everyone knows.
Stars peep out from their cozy beds,
Here comes the night with dreams in threads.

Naughty owls hoot, making quite a fuss,
While crickets chirp, riding on the bus.
Streetlamps flicker like butterflies' wings,
Nightfall giggles, and sweetly sings.

Moonlight bathes all in a silver hue,
Creepy shadows that might scare you!
But laughing ghosts float through the trees,
No one can frown in such a breeze!

Under the blanket of starlit skies,
Everyone whispers their tiny lies.
Nightfall's charm brings glimmers of cheer,
Where worries vanish, and joy draws near.

Beneath the Mistletoe's Gentle Gaze

A sprig of green hangs with style and flair,
Kissing at Christmas, do we dare?
Tommy's cheeks turn bright as a rose,
While Sally giggles and crunches her toes.

A partridge in a pear tree sings sweet,
But under mistletoe, you must face defeat!
Awkward hugs, and cheeks so red,
Is it love or just holiday spread?

Elves conspire with a winking glance,
For under the mistletoe, there's little chance.
Laughter echoes, surrounding the banter,
All in good fun, that holiday canter!

Santa rolls by in a sleigh full of cheer,
With rosy cheeks and a belly to steer.
Mistletoe magic, with giggles and light,
Nothing's more silly than love at first sight!

The Hushed Serenade of Frosty Pines

In the still of night, the pines stand tall,
Whispering secrets, they hear it all.
With snowflakes tumbling like cotton candies,
Their frozen limbs just shift and dandy.

Frosty winds hum a chilly tune,
As rabbits hop beneath the moon.
Squirrels chatter, planning their feast,
In the frosty pines, they're never least!

Icicles jingle like tiny bells,
Their frosted charm casts magical spells.
Nature's laughter fills the air,
In winter's hush, we dance without care.

So grab your friends, no time to fret,
In frosty pines, let's make a duet!
With giggles and glee, we weave our song,
In this winter world, we all belong.

A Celebration of Twinkling Eyes

When you catch my eye, oh what a sight,
Like a disco ball under the moonlight.
They twinkle and sparkle, a mischievous tease,
Making my heart dance, oh, if you please.

In the awkward silences, your glance is a cue,
Like a cat plotting suddenly to pounce on its stew.
Those twinkling eyes hold a universe wide,
A confetti explosion I just can't hide.

A wink here, a blink there, oh what a game,
Playing pin-the-tail on the forgetful brain.
With every flutter, my giggles increase,
Like a soda bottle that just can't find peace.

So here's to the twinkles that spark up our day,
Making mundane moments a wild cabaret.
In a world full of frowns, let our laughter arise,
For joy's just as bright as your twinkling eyes!

Wishes Like Snowflakes in Flight

Wishes come down like snowflakes afloat,
Landing on dreams, in a whimsical boat.
Some big, some small, all fluffy and white,
Each one a giggle, pure magic in flight.

I wished for a cat that dances with flair,
Or maybe a spoon that knows how to share.
Wishes like snowflakes can shimmer and glow,
Swirling and twirling, just letting them flow.

Let's catch them together, a flurry of hopes,
Building a castle where every wish gropes.
With laughter as bricks, we'll make it quite grand,
A kingdom of whimsy where we can just stand.

So I'll scoop up these wishes, let them take flight,
Like a snowstorm of joy on a cold winter's night.
In this frosty dreamland where nothing is wrong,
Wishes like snowflakes will carry our song!

The Serendipity of Heartfelt Moments

Stumbling through life like a cat on a wall,
I find awesome moments, like a soft-spoken call.
The duck in the park quacking silly good cheer,
Reminds me that laughter should be held dear.

Serendipity strikes like lightning, oh hush,
When you trip on your feet, or land in a rush.
A moment so funny, it makes your heart race,
Like slipping in mud, what a glorious place!

Found treasure in laughter from a friend's silly face,
Like tripping on sunshine while dancing in space.
These moments are gold, oh they sparkle and shine,
They bubble up joy like an odd glass of wine.

So here's to mischief and joy that we find,
In the everyday dance and the playful unwind.
Let's raise a toast to the giggles we see,
In the serendipity of life, wild and free!

Countdowns Echoing in the Stillness

Tick-tock goes the clock, like a dancer in shoes,
Counting the seconds when nothing's the news.
The echo of silence, a loud whispers' feat,
Like waiting for cookies to come from the heat.

Five, four, three, oh where did it go?
Time's slipping away like a soft little glow.
In moments so quiet, my thoughts start to race,
Visualizing cupcakes, icing, and lace.

With every countdown, the tension does climb,
Counting the giggles, oh isn't it prime?
Down to the last, what will it unveil?
Like balloons in the air or a well-timed fail.

So let's lose ourselves in these echoes of time,
Savoring laughter, our joy is the rhyme.
In the stillness, we'll ponder and spark,
Count down our moments, ignite the heart's arc!

The Heartstrings of Holiday Memory

When grandma danced with glee,
The cat flew up a tree,
A turkey fell on the floor,
And we laughed till we were sore.

With mistletoe on the door,
We kissed the dog—oh, what a chore!
The cookies burned, the smoke alarm,
Yet still, we felt the holiday charm.

Uncle's jokes make no real sense,
A snowman's built with no defense,
He melts away as we all cheer,
For joy and laughter bring us near.

So raise a glass, let's reminisce,
With every hug and silly kiss,
These heartstrings pull, they intertwine,
In holiday tales, we all align.

Carols Woven in Frosty Air

The snowflakes tap-dance in delight,
While squirrels hold a choir night,
The reindeer giggle as they glide,
With a frosty air, we're filled with pride.

Carolers croon off-key with glee,
The neighbors shout, 'Oh, let it be!'
A cat joins in with a fierce meow,
The whole street laughs, it's the talk of the town.

Jingle bells ring, but so do we,
In long johns singing, 'Set me free!'
The snowman winks with a carrot nose,
As friendly snowball fights compose.

So let us sing and dance with cheer,
For in this moment, joy is here,
With every note, let laughter soar,
In frosty air, we can't ignore.

The Enchantment of Glowing Embers

Crackling logs and stories old,
We roast our marshmallows 'til they fold,
The fire spins a magical tale,
While socks are left to set the sail.

A raccoon sneaks in for a bite,
We chase him off, what a funny sight!
As shadows dance upon the walls,
We laugh till we hear the ember calls.

Hot cocoa spills down my chin,
A joy-filled face, where to begin?
With every sip, our spirits rise,
In glowing embers, laughter flies.

So gather 'round, let's share the glow,
With silly hats in a warm, soft flow,
In every flicker, we find our bliss,
In this enchantment, we reminisce.

A Love Note to the Night Sky

Oh, twinkle stars, you cosmic peeps,
You light my dreams and help me sleep,
Yet offer only giggles like a show,
As UFOs fly by, too fast to know.

The moon grins wide, what a bright face,
Who knew he'd have such a joyful grace?
Caught his shine in my cereal bowl,
A breakfast dance for our hungry souls.

Galaxies spin, making us sway,
While comets zoom like kids at play,
"It's a shooting star!" I yell with glee,
As my cat naps, oblivious to me.

So here's my note, dear sky up high,
With every laugh, let our spirits fly,
In starry nights, so wild and free,
Love's simple notes are magic, you see?

Milton Keynes UK
Ingram Content Group UK Ltd.
UKHW020700021224
3298UKWH00039B/311